40 DAYS AND

OF

FASTING

Written by Mya Sanders

MyaSandersBooks.com

Dedicated to My Family and Friends Who Never Gave Up on Me

First Edition: [February 2020]
Printed in the United States of America
ISBN: [978191028534]

CONTENTS	Pages

Contents..3

Introduction..6

What is Fasting?..7

Why Fast?..9

Day 1...12

Day 2...15

Day 3...17

Day 4...20

Day 5...23

Day 6...25

Day 7...28

Day 8...31

Day 9...34

Day 10...36

Day 11...38

Day 12...40

Day 13...42

Day 14...45

Day 15..47

Day 16..50

Day 17..53

Day 18..56

Day 19..59

Day 20..61

Day 21..63

Day 22..66

Day 23..69

Day 24..71

Day 25..73

Day 26..76

Day 27..79

Day 28..82

Day 29..84

Day 30..86

Day 31..88

Day 32..91

Day 33..94

Day 34..96

Day 35..98

Day 36..100

Day 37..102

Day 38..104

Day 39..106

Day 40..109

Smoothies..111

Testimonies..117

INTRODUCTION

I will never forget that season in my life when I first fasted for 40 days and 40 nights. I desired to be used by God and be delivered from constant tormenting spirits. Additionally, I wanted to be a soul winner for God's Kingdom. I cried out to God in the agony "Lord, use me. I want to do more for you. Deliver me so I can help others with my testimony. Show me all my purposes for my life."

As I journeyed through the 40 days and 40 nights of fasting and prayer, I received revelations beyond human imagination. As I studied God's Word and listened to him speak to me regarding my life, I was being changed from glory to glory. As a gift of seeing and transporting, all the gifts that God has given me were heighten during these days and afterwards. Only God gets the glory when he allows me visions and supernatural visitations. These experiences I want to share, for I believe that you too want to be used by God. And perhaps you share the same gifts.

Join me as I take you through this true extraordinary experience that I had during those 40 days and 40 nights of fasting and prayer.

What is Fasting?

Fasting is a voluntarily act of refraining from food and/or water. It is essentially giving up food (or something else) for a period of time in order to focus your thoughts on God. But as for me, when they were sick, my clothing was sackcloth: I humbled my soul with fasting; and my prayer returned into mine own bosom (Psalm 35:13).

There are many different fasts. During a regular fast, we refrain from all food and drink except water. And when he had fasted forty days and forty nights, he afterwards and hungered (Matthew 4:2). In partial fast, we omit a certain meal each day and strictly restrict the quantity of food and drink we consume. I ate no delicacies, no meat or wine entered my mouth (Daniels 10:3). In a complete fast, we do not eat or drink liquid of any kind. This fast should not go on for more than three days. Neither eat nor drink three nights and days. (Ester 4:16).

In a supernatural fast, as in the case of Moses, who abstained from both food and water for forty days (enabled to do so only by a miraculous enabling from God). Then I abode in the mount forty days and forty nights, I neither did eat bread nor drink water (Deuteronomy 9:9).

A liquid fast is a partial fast that allows liquids of all kinds to be taken for any period of time (juice, broth or beverages). All fasts can be modified depending on pregnancy and other physical elements.

You may also wish to fast from all food for only a particular meal each day. In other words, you may choose to skip lunch for a day or two or a week, or dinner, or even breakfast. All such forms of partial fasting are entirely appropriate. If it is easy for you to give up something, then it's not a sacrifice.

One of the most telling passages in which fasting is mentioned is Matthew 6:16, where Jesus is teaching His disciples basic principles of godly living. When speaking on fasting, He begins with, "When you fast," not "If you fast." Jesus' words imply that fasting will be a regular practice in His followers' lives.

Why Fast?

Preparation for Ministry: Jesus spent 40 days and nights in the wilderness fasting and praying before He began God's work on this earth. He needed time alone to prepare for what His Father had called Him to do (Matthew 4:1-17; Mark 1:12-13; Luke 4:1-14).

To seek and consult wisdom from God: Fast to hear an answer from GOD through prayer. Paul and Barnabas prayed and fasted for the elders of the churches before committing them to the Lord for His service (Acts 14:23).

To express grief: Nehemiah mourned, fasted, and prayed when he learned Jerusalem's walls had been broken down, leaving the Israelites vulnerable and disgraced (Nehemiah 1:1-4).

For deliverance and protection: Ezra declared a corporate fast and prayed for a safe journey for the Israelites as they made the 900 mile journey to Jerusalem from Babylon (Ezra 8:21-23).

For Repentance: After Jonah pronounced judgment against the city of Nineveh, the king covered himself with sackcloth and sat in the dust. He then ordered the people to fast and pray. Jonah 3:10 says, "When God saw what they did and how they turned from their evil ways, He relented and did not bring on them the destruction He had threatened."

To gain victory: After losing 40,000 men in battle in two days, the Israelites cried out to God for help. Judges 20:26 says all the people went up to Bethel and "sat weeping before the Lord." They also "fasted that day until evening." The next day the Lord gave them victory over the Benjamites.

I picked the liquid fast for my first 40 days and 40 nights of fasting. I will be sharing my experience and revelations as I receive from the God from my first day to the fortieth day.

I thank the Lord, Jesus Christ, for giving me this opportunity to share my experiences.

Your Experience

DAY 1

(Isaiah 58:6)

"Is not this the fast that I have chosen? To loosen the bands of wickedness, to undo the heavy burdens, and to let the oppressed go free, and that ye break every yoke?"

For maximum spiritual benefit, I suggest to set aside ample time to be with the Lord. Listen for His leading. The more time you spend with Him the more meaningful your fast will be.

I am really excited about my 40 days and 40nights fast! This is my first day, so I am very energized, and it feels like any other day. I was anxious to know what God has in store for me for the duration of the 40days fast. I knew God will deliver me from somethings and have me closer to him during these days.

I began my day in praise and worship. Read and meditate on God's word. I Invited the Holy Spirit to take me over, and to do His good pleasure. For it is God which worketh in you both to will and to do of his good pleasure (Philippians 2:13). I prayed that Jesus would use me and show me how to influence my world, my family, my church, my community, my country and beyond.

Additionally, I spent time praying for strength to complete the 40 days fast and achieve goals at the end of the fast. And he said unto me, my grace is sufficient for thee: for my strength is made perfect in weakness.

Most gladly therefore will I rather glory in my infirmities, that the power of Christ may rest upon me (2 Corinthians 12:9-10).

I had 12 cups of water and 3 cups of green tea.

YOUR EXPERIENCE

DAY 2

(Matthew 4:4)

"But he answered and said, It is written, Man shall not live by bread alone, but by every word that proceedeth out of the mouth of God"

Still excited, especially since temptation came much quicker than my last 3 day fast. I was near my mother's house and just stopped by without any notice. My mom happened to make my favorite dish, lasagna (type of wide, flat pasta, commonly refers to an Italian cuisine dish made with stacked layers of this flat). My mother said she just felt like making lasagna today. I laughed at the enemy and said well unfortunately I cannot eat it because I am on a fast. There hath no temptation taken you but such as is common to man: but God is faithful, who will not suffer you to be tempted above that ye are able; but will with the temptation also make a way to escape, that ye may be able to bear it (1Corinthians 10:13). She understood and quickly put away the food, after which we talked for about two hours.

This temptation proves that GOD is going to do something wonderful. Because you know that the testing of your faith produces perseverance (James 1:3).

I had 12 cups of water, 2 cups of green tea with honey, and one green smoothie. I rehearsed 5 dance songs that I choreographed for two hours for my fitness.

YOUR EXPERIENCE

DAY 3

(Deuteronomy 33:27)

"The eternal God is thy refuge, and underneath are the everlasting arms: and he shall thrust out the enemy from before thee; and shall say, Destroy them."

Today being the third day of my fast, I was feeling pretty good especially thinking of the previous test which I passed. Today in prayer, I went into spiritual warfare and demons tried to talk to me and said "You think your praying is working but it's not." That's when I knew it was destroying the works of the enemy because the demons were trying to get me to stop. I prayed louder and yelled louder "Do not talk to me! I did not give you permission to speak to me! You have no authority over my life and anyone I am connected to. Take your hands off my marriage, my husband, my family, my friends and everyone I am connected to. In as much then as the children have partaken of flesh and blood, He Himself likewise shared in the same, that through death He might destroy him who had the power of death, that is, the devil, 15 and release those who through fear of death were all their lifetime subject to bondage (Hebrews 2:14-15).

I yelled, "I am tired of you Satan. You have failed and I will never give up on what GOD has promised me. You will return everything you stolen from me or anything you have from my ancestors as well. Give it all back! It is mine in Jesus' Name!

I saw a major demon charging me in the spirit and Then I yelled, " Stop, Get out my way". It flew back as I yelled and disappeared. Submit yourselves, then, to God. Resist the devil, and he will flee from you (James 4:7). I have a new energy, boldness, and strength today.

I had 18 cups of water and 2 cups of hot coco. I danced praise and worship of random Christian songs for 3 hours.

YOUR EXPERIENCE

DAY 4

(2 Corinthians 5:8)

"We are confident, I say, and would prefer to be away from the body and at home with the Lord."

Today in prayer, I went to heaven. I have been to heaven before and am always excited when I go. It's an overwhelming feeling of surrender before I leave. Praying in tongues, always leads me into a supernatural experience. But you, beloved, building yourselves up in your most holy faith and praying in the Holy Spirit (Jude 1:20). I was praying in tongues, and it's a point that the holy spirit completely takes me over and that's when I leave. For anyone who speaks in a tongue does not speak to people but to God. Indeed, no one understands them; they utter mysteries by the Spirit (1 Corinthians 14:2).

In heaven, I was kneeling at the feet of GOD and Jesus was on the right hand of the father. Set your hearts on things above, where Christ is, seated at the right hand of God (Colossians 3:1). Even though my head was still bowed, I still saw Jesus come into GOD as one being. GOD told me to rise, "Rise my daughter, my Mya" and I did.

Every time I visit heaven, I feel an overwhelming love and peace. I have more knowledge of things when I am there. For now, we see only a reflection as in a mirror; then we shall see face to face. Now I know in part; then I shall know fully, even as I am fully known (1 Corinthians 13:12).

We were walking through heaven as he spoke to me. I saw mansions in the distance and levels of Heaven. There were angels all around God and many that followed us. I do not remember everything what GOD said but I know it will be knowledge that I will need in the future. It was shared with me in 2020. It seemed like days went by and suddenly, I was back on earth.

I had 14 cups of water and 2 cups of green tea. I danced to praise and worship of random Christian songs for 3 hours.

YOUR EXPERIENCE

DAY 5

(Ephesians 1:18)

"I pray that the eyes of your heart may be enlightened, so that you will know what is the hope of His calling, what are the riches of the glory of His inheritance in the saints."

Still on the fast, GOD reminded me of a time when I woke up but I couldn't see anything. I thought it was a dream, but I was not asleep, because I could remember waking up. I immediately cried out to GOD to let me see. Then GOD said, " I am giving you new eyes to see. I am here and will always be." Then I fell back to sleep. And surely I am with you always, to the very end of the age (Matthew 28:20).

I woke up again but with a new pair of eyes much better than the previous. I saw colors more vivid and had a new appreciation for nature as I took a four mile walk outside.

I saw different colored leaves (orange, brown, yellow colors). The blue sky filled with white clouds and a huge angel hoovering over me in the sky while I walked along the path. Additionally, I had my three angels that were assigned to me from birth traveling with us. Are not all angels ministering spirits sent to serve those who will inherit salvation? (Hebrews 1:14).

I also believe that day I was given another level of discernment.

I did a little warm up, cardio, and cool down routine I made up while teaching a dance class for one hour.

YOUR EXPERIENCE

DAY 6

1 Corinthians 10:13

"No temptation has overtaken you except what is common to mankind. And God is faithful; he will not let you be tempted beyond what you can bear. But when you are tempted, he will also provide a way out so that you can endure it".

Today was another food temptation. My husband came home with my favorite kind of pizza. He said he ordered it fresh, especially for me just the way I liked it. With my face frowned, I thanked him for the idea and reminded him that I was still on my fast. He apologized and said, "I guess more for me and laughed as he ate a slice." Run from temptations that capture young people. Always do the right thing. Be faithful, loving, and easy to get along with. Worship with people whose hearts are pure (2 Timothy 2:22).

As I ran to our bedroom to pray, I could smell the aroma of the pizza fill the entire house. The smell was stronger than usual or was the temptation stronger. Regardless, I made it again that day without eating anything. I asked my husband to freeze me two slices, so it could be an award when the fast was over. He did and it was the best pizza I ever ate! I was proud of myself resisting the devil again. For we do not have a high priest who is unable to empathize with our weaknesses, but we have one who has been tempted in every way, just as we are—yet he did not sin (Hebrews 4:15).

Though it was not easy going through all this, but I was determined to achieve GOD's purpose for my life, which is what kept me going.

YOUR EXPERIENCE

DAY 7

(Galatians 6:8)

"For the one who sows to his own flesh will from the flesh reap corruption, but the one who sows to the Spirit will from the Spirit reap eternal life."

On the 7th day, I visited heaven again. I arrived face to face with GOD. Even though, I didn't see his face clearly but only saw a bright warm loving light. He takes me to a new and different level in heaven that I have never been before. At this level, I saw a room filled with gold, rubies, diamonds, jewels, and different precious stones. GOD told me that as a result of my obedience, I will have a portion of it set up just like in heaven on earth. The twelve gates were twelve pearls, each gate made of a single pearl. The great street of the city was of gold, as pure as transparent glass (Revelation 21:21).

Suddenly, I saw five trucks filled with gold as they traveled through the atmosphere on their way to earth for me. I was really happy because I knew that the financial miracle that I have been waiting on to my family, friends, and more. For bodily discipline is only of little profit, but godliness is profitable for all things, since it holds promise for the present life and also for the life to come (1 Timothy 4:8).

I thanked GOD for the awesome reward and was back on earth. That day was filled with wonderful surprises which made me think that the gold was not really gold but perhaps something else? When I asked God about it, he said, "My treasures in Heaven can be anything I want them to be. But you will receive your financial miracle as well....it's on the way without no delays." Then I saw a vision of two of the trucks still in the atmosphere on their path to earth. I am starting to understand that I can not rush God and need his perfect timing in every aspect of my life.

I had 12 cups of water, 3 cups of coco, and one green smoothie. I danced to praise and worship of random Christian songs for 3 hours.

YOUR EXPERIENCE

DAY 8

(Matthew 19:14-16)

"But when Jesus saw it, he was indignant and said to them, "Let the children come to me; do not hinder them, for to such belongs the kingdom of God. Truly, I say to you, whoever does not receive the kingdom of God like a child shall not enter it." And he took them in his arms and blessed them, laying his hands on them."

Today, I visited heaven again, and as usual, I was very excited. But this visit was going to be very emotional. I was filled with overwhelming joy of what my experience will be this time. I arrived standing on a level in heaven where children were playing. Jesus was in front of me and children began to gather around, talking, and all I felt was their love, but I was feeling their love for me too. These children loved me.

I felt some of the children were my children. There were a few I lost and maybe some that were not conceived yet. They had been playing together. A good person leaves an inheritance for their children's children, but a sinner's wealth is stored up for the righteous (Proverbs 13:22).

In the far distant, in a different area, I saw my ancestors. Even though, I never met them before, I knew who they were. When I got back to earth, I did not remember what the children said but I knew they were words of encouragement and love. I had carried it with me as if I was carrying all of them. I felt pregnant and God said, "You are pregnant with purpose. Some things you carry is not only for yourself."

I had 14 cups of water, 1 cup of coco, and 3 cups of green tea. I later did my warm up, cardio, and cool down routine I made up while teaching a dance class earlier in the year. It is usually one hour.

YOUR EXPERIENCE

DAY 9

(James 1:12)

"Blessed is the one who perseveres under trial because, having stood the test, that person will receive the crown of life that the Lord has promised to those who love him."

On the 9th day of my fast, I visited heaven again. I saw my future self in heaven. I was beautiful, but not the beauty on earth. I had many crowns and mantels on my head, I was dressed in a royal garment with colors of purple, rainbow, and non-earthly colors. Colors that do not exist on earth. I had metal rewards on my shoulders as in the military. Henceforth there is laid up for me a crown of righteousness, which the Lord, the righteous judge, shall give me at that day: and not to me only, but unto all them also that love his appearing (2 Timothy 4:8)

Immediately I returned to earth with relief and peace. I felt like a different person. While continuing to pray, something broke off of me. I am not sure what kind of demon it was but I felt it come off me.

I had 10 cups of water and 1 smoothie. I rehearsed 5 songs that choreographed for two hours for my fitness.

YOUR EXPERIENCE

DAY 10

(Matthew 11:28-30)

"Come to me, all you who are weary and burdened, and I will give you rest. Take my yoke upon you and learn from me, for I am gentle and humble in heart, and you will find rest for your souls. For my yoke is easy and my burden is light."

Today, Jesus visited me. I was dancing before the lord in my house. But sat down as I was overwhelmed with sadness for my godson who passed. I closed my eyes and I saw angels filled the room. Then I saw Jesus above my head as I was sitting down. I could not see his face, but there was fire in his eyes. The hair on his head was white like wool, as white as snow, and his eyes were like blazing fire (Revelation 1:14).

I am not sure why I see clearer with my natural eyes shut than open. Perhaps, it is the nature of sin while looking through my natural eyes? Jesus told me to give him all of my burdens. I began to sob with rushing tears and said, "I can't, I am in so much pain Lord." Jesus asked me again to give it to him. I opened my eyes and gave him everything I was holding on. Cast your cares on the LORD and he will sustain you; he will never let the righteous be shaken (Psalms 55:22). I closed my eyes again and began to pray.

Then his presence left me. But I was given peace and strength. I had 10 cups of water, 1 cup of tea, and a smoothie.

YOUR EXPERIENCE

DAY 11

(John 15:1-27)

"I am the true vine, and my Father is the vinedresser. Every branch in me that does not bear fruit he takes away, and every branch that does bear fruit he prunes, that it may bear more fruit. Already you are clean because of the word that I have spoken to you. Abide in me, and I in you. As the branch cannot bear fruit by itself, unless it abides in the vine, neither can you, unless you abide in me. I am the vine; you are the branches. Whoever abides in me and I in him, he it is that bears much fruit, for apart from me you can do nothing."

Today as I was praying, GOD showed me a green tree in my throat as I was praising his name and then there was fire. I asked GOD what both elements meant. Then GOD told me, "You will continue to bear fruit and I will burn up the bad fruit in your life. The fruit that is not growing, but taking up space, weighing you down."

I had 12 cups of water and 1 cup of smoothie. I walked 4 miles today.

YOUR EXPERIENCE

DAY 12:

(Ephesians 6:12-13)

"For we do not wrestle against flesh and blood, but against principalities, against powers, against the rulers of the darkness of this age, against spiritual hosts of wickedness in the heavenly places. Therefore, take up the whole armor of God, that you may be able to withstand in the evil day, and having done all, to stand."

Today, my husband and I were watching a movie called "Kung Fu Hustle". In one of the scenes, GOD spoke to me. The landlady stepped in front of her husband as two men were playing stringed instruments that released swords. The swords were invisible to the audience at first, then we saw the swords, finally we saw demons throwing the swords.

The landlady stopped the swords and demons by yelling out a roar called the "Lion's roar". GOD told me to continue to pray for my husband and remember I do not wrestle against flesh and blood (Ephesians 6:12-13). If I continue to yell out his name and speak in the authority that he has given me than no weapon formed against me will prosper and there is no need to fear never again. No weapon formed against you shall prosper, And every tongue which rises against you in judgment You shall condemn (Isaiah 55:17).

I had 12 cups of water, 2 cups of green tea with honey, and one green smoothie. I rehearsed 5 songs that choreographed for two hours for my fitness.

YOUR EXPERIENCE

DAY 13

(Deuteronomy 28:12-13)

"The Lord will open to you His good treasure, the heavens, to give the rain to your land in its season, and to bless all the work of your hand. You shall lend to many nations, but you shall not borrow. And the Lord will make you the head and not the tail; you shall be above only, and not be beneath, if you heed the commandments of the Lord your God, which I command you today, and are careful to observe them."

Today, I saw a vision of a check in the mail. While waiting in expectant of good news, instead, I received a bill from the IRS (Internal Revenue Service), stating that we owe $2,000 for city taxes. The enemy loves to lie and trick people into thinking the opposite of what GOD said. We haven't lived in the main city for four years.

I immediately started praying, "Lord, please help us. You said we should call on you in our time of need and we need you now Lord. Call upon Me in the day of trouble; I will deliver you, and you shall glorify Me (Psalms 50:15). We are to be lenders and not borrowers (Deuteronomy 28:12-13) Lord please fix this so that your word will come to pass".

So it was revealed that my husband forgot to update his new address of work. So we would not owe city taxes. I called the city tax department and explained to them. They told me to have my husband update his address at work, send his and my Michigan IDs, and copies of our W2's; which I did. The system do not want to let you go, but you can demand to get out the system and get on GOD's system. And my God shall supply all your needs according to His riches in glory by Christ Jesus (Philippians 4:19)

Two weeks later, I received a letter from the city tax department clearing us from all past due taxes. Two weeks later, I received a refund check.

I drank 14 cups of water and 1 cup of green tea. I danced to praise and worship of random Christian songs for 3hours.

YOUR EXPERIENCE

DAY 14

(Isaiah 41:10)

"Fear thou not; for I [am] with thee: be not dismayed; for I [am] thy God: I will strengthen thee; yea, I will help thee; yea, I will uphold thee with the right hand of my righteousness."

Today, I heard my godson speak to me. I was in prayer and was missing my godson, Klyn. He said, *"Hi godmom, I don't have a lot of time to speak to you. GOD will only allow me to talk to you for a limited time. There is so much knowledge I have and so much more I can do now. I 'm so happy and full of love earthly words cannot explain. I love you and mom. Please remind her for me."*

I realized today that my husband and I have a new marriage. All I can say is that GOD did it. We are like newlyweds!

Today, I almost fainted. I was walking in the hallway in my house and I saw black for a quick second and I immediately called out "Jesus". For "whoever calls on the name of the Lord shall be saved" (Romans 10:13). My sight restored and I sat down. I guess those detox teas really worked but probably took the sugar intake that I needed.

I had 12 cups of water and 2 cups of detox tea. I also drank 2 cups of smoothie and felt better for the rest of the day.

YOUR EXPERIENCE

DAY 15

(Ephesians 5:30-33)

"For we are members of His body, of His flesh and of His bones. "For this reason a man shall leave his father and mother and be joined to his wife, and the two shall become one flesh. "This is a great mystery, but I speak concerning Christ and the church. Nevertheless, let each one of you in particular so love his own wife as himself, and let the wife see that she respects her husband."

Today, GOD told me to pray for my marriage with a positive attitude. He said I should treat my husband as I treat him. GOD said, "When I ask you do something you do not roll your eyes. You don't sigh. You don't ask why." Now I have a different attitude towards serving my husband. This is one of the most debated and misunderstood roles of being a spouse. In (Colossians 3:18-19) the bible says "other halves, be difficulty to your husbands, as is fitting within the Lord." But, submission has nothing to do with blind obedience or girls being not as good as men. It has greater role to play with the wife entrusting herself to her husband. Submission is going hand in hand with the husband's function of management.

The wife offers the husband the opportunity to be the chief that God desires him to be and satisfy the roles of a husband in a biblical marriage. God made female to be man's help meet. Inside the Bible, the phrase "helper" is used to consult Eve, at some point of advent, and God himself.

This means that being a helper comes with fantastic strength. It encourages the wife's duty to assist the husband in becoming all that God needs him to be. In the same manner, God facilitates us to grow into who he desires us to be.

In Ephesians 5:33, the bible commands wives to respect their husbands. This means revering, admiring and honoring their husbands. An amazing spouse values her husband's reviews, admires his values and individual, and is thoughtful of his wishes, which includes the want for self-worth and the desire to be wanted.

I drank 13 cups of water and 3 cups of smoothie. I rehearsed 5 songs that choreographed for two hours for my fitness.

YOUR EXPERIENCE

DAY 16

(Ezekiel 18:4)

"Behold, all souls are Mine; the soul of the father as well as the soul of the son is Mine; the soul who sins shall die."

Today, I asked from God in prayer, why some demons leave when we pray and others when we pray and fast? The Lord said because there are different ranks of demons. Depending on the level of a demon, fasting is needed to totally get delivered from it because there must be a sacrifice made.

While I was praying in tongues, a demon separated itself from me, it was attached to me some how but it was not inside of my spirit. Only the Holy Spirit lives in my spirit and demons can not go inside where his presence is. But because of the sinful body, demons can attach themselves on the outer. I praised God for deliverance because am totally free. It was a soul tie.

As soon as it left me, I got a text from an unrecognized phone number. I believe it was my ex boyfriend. I never responded and blocked the number. Soul ties account for the influences that they have on each other involved in it. You might not see them, but you can see the results.

Soul ties usually happen between two people who become intimate not necessarily physical. For example, there might be someone who manipulates you and therefore, that's a soul tie. Anything or anyone who can influence you in a negative way. In Genesis 2:24, God said "marriage spouses become one flesh and not one soul". Therefore, God is against all soul ties. My soul belongs to Lord and my body belongs to my husband only. and you are of Christ, and Christ is of God (1 Corinthians 3:23).

I drank 18 cups of water, 2 cups of green tea. I did 50 sit ups, 20 jumping jacks and walked for one hour.

YOUR EXPERIENCE

DAY 17

(Psalms 138:7)

"Though I walk in the midst of trouble, thou wilt revive me: thou shalt stretch forth thine hand against the wrath of mine enemies, and thy right hand shall save me."

Today, marking the 17th day of my fast, I went to hell. I was in a boat invisible to the demons. I was traveling on a river of blood and inside this river were bones. I saw demons on the land plotting and planning about humans.

Some demons looked at the river and I was still invisible until GOD spoke to me to tell me my instructions. The boat stopped and GOD told me to reach in the river. The demons were now allowed to see me, they started making noises and heading toward me quickly. I reached down in the river and picked up a treasure box that was royal blue and carved with black markings. Inside the box was my healing gift. I cried out to GOD, please save me because the demons are getting closer. Behold, the LORD's hand is not shortened, That it cannot save; Nor His ear heavy, That it cannot hear. But your iniquities have separated you from your God; And your sins have hidden *His* face from you (Isaiah 59:1)

Immediately, the top opened up with a bright light and one hand came down and lifted me up. I was back in my body at home thanking GOD for my gift of healing that the enemy has stolen and was hiding from me. My times are in Your hand; Deliver me from the hand of my enemies and from those who persecute me (Psalms 31:15).

I continue to see my marriage changing for the good. We spend more time praying together and he even spends time alone with GOD. He shut off his game after one hour of playing and if that's not a miracle I do not know what it is. He usually plays the game for 3 hours at least.

I had 14 cups of water and 2 cups of green tea. I did my warm, cardio, and cool down routine I made up while teaching a dance class earlier this year. It is usually one hour.

YOUR EXPERIENCE

DAY 18

(2 Samuel 6:11-12)

"You turned my wailing into dancing; you removed my sackcloth and clothed me with joy, that my heart may sing your praises and not be silent. Lord my God, I will praise you forever."

Today, I was reminded of the vision GOD gave me concerning my dance ministry. I was dancing outside in front of thousands of people on stage. There is a band and singers. It was a warm and sunny day. There were four other dancers with me on stage. We just finished praise dancing and now we were entering worship dance.

Dance is noted on many occasions in the Scripture. The primary look of God's people dancing is an act of worship found in Exodus 15:20: "Miriam the prophetess, Aaron's sister, took a tambourine in her hand, and all of the women accompanied her, with tambourines and dancing." This comfortable dance to the Lord, led by Miriam, followed Israel's crossing of the pink Sea and celebrated Israel's newfound freedom from slavery. But, dancing was not always provided in a good light inside the Bible.

Soon after Miriam's dance of praise, the Israelites had been determined dancing earlier than a golden calf in worship. "While Moses approached the camp and saw the calf and the dancing, his anger burned and he threw the tablets out of his hands, breaking them to pieces at the foot of the mountain" (Exodus 32:19). On this event dancing changed into part of a depraved, idolatrous carousal.

Accordingly, dancing is a method of expression that may be used properly or for evil. There are different dancing within the Bible which include (2 Samuel 6:16), which has David "jumping and dancing." Also, the Amalekites danced in celebration after plundering Judah and Philistia (I Samuel 30:16); Theirs was a short-lived dance, but, as David and his men quickly defeated them (verses 17-20). As long as dance is worship to Jesus, God-focused, and praiseworthy, it has a proper place in worship.

I drank 10 cups of water, 2 cups of green tea, and 1 cup of smoothie. I walked two miles today.

YOUR EXPERIENCE

DAY 19

(Proverbs 3:5)

"Trust in the Lord with all your heart, and do not lean on your own understanding."

Today I was reminded of a vision. I once had a vision, about a celebrity dying because she raised up a demon. GOD told me, "People are foolish when they allow the enemy to trick them into thinking the things of the world will last. People call on (put their faith and trust) so many things besides me." The Lord is my strength and my shield; in him my heart trusts, and I am helped; my heart exults, and with my song I give thanks to him (Psalm 28:7).

This world will end and heaven will come down to have a new earth. It will return how I originally created it. Then I saw "a new heaven and a new earth," for the first heaven and the first earth had passed away, and there was no longer any sea. I saw the Holy City, the new Jerusalem, coming down out of heaven from God (Revelation 21:1-2). It got me thinking about how fame, money, and status really doesn't matter. I felt sad for the celebrities who believed the lie and prayed that some will confess their sins and ask Jesus to come into their hearts. God said, "Some have already committed the unforgiveable sin and therefore they will not be saved." And then he gave me a few celebrities' names to pray for.

I drank 13 cups of water and 3 cups of smoothie. I rehearsed 5 songs that choreographed for two hours for my fitness.

YOUR EXPERIENCE

DAY 20

(2 Corinthians 1:20)

For as many as are the promises of God, in Him they are yes; therefore also through Him is our Amen to the glory of God through us.

Today I was reminded of my daughter's vision. She was beautiful. She was almost two years old. She had two dimples like me and smooth milk chocolate skin with curly hair. I thought "I need to comb her hair." Her hair was messy as if she just jumped out of bed. She was still in her pajamas as she sat at the kitchen table eating cereal.

A drop of milk fell from her two tone lips and she sucked it back into her mouth. I giggled and thought to myself "You want to make sure you get every drop." The Lord said "Remember I am not a man to lie. You will become a mother, my daughter". And being fully assured that what God had promised, He was able also to perform (Romans 4:21).

God reminded me again when he renamed me Sarah and gave me her mantel. I am Mother of Nations. I will bless her and will surely give you a son by her. I will bless her so that she will be the mother of nations; kings of peoples will come from her (Genesis 17:16).

I drank 14 cups of water and 3 cups of green tea. I danced two hours today for praise and worship.

YOUR EXPERIENCE

DAY 21:

(Matthew 7:21-23)

"Not everyone who says to me, 'Lord, Lord,' will enter the kingdom of heaven, but only the one who does the will of my Father who is in heaven. Many will say to me on that day, 'Lord, Lord, did we not prophesy in your name and in your name drive out demons and in your name perform many miracles?' Then I will tell them plainly, 'I never knew you. Away from me, you evildoers!"

Today, I went to hell again and saw different prisons. Each prison had a title on top of each: False prophets, pastors, dancers, singers, athletes, etc. They were crying out, "Help me. I don't belong here. Please tell Jesus." Some people were working by building chains and different objects. (Matthew 7:21-23).   Some people were burning. I felt anguished, and angry. I saw people who were good people but did not access Jesus Christ as Lord. I would look at them and see their entire life. It was truly sad and heart breaking. Jesus answered, "I am the way and the truth and the life. No one comes to the Father except through me. (John 14:6)

I got back to earth and Jesus shared his heart. It was never GOD's will to have anyone in hell but because of the gift of choice, we did not choose him. It hurt Jesus beyond words and it grieved him. I couldn't stop crying and asked for repentance because I never knew that GOD told me to pray for a particular singer a week ago and I just thought it was my imagination. So I had to repent for not praying for him like he said. So now I continue to pray for him and anyone that GOD drops in my spirit.

I had 14 cups of water and 2 cups of green tea. I did my warm, cardio, and cool down routine I made up while teaching a dance class earlier this year. It is usually one hour.

YOUR EXPERIENCE

DAY 22

(Deuteronomy 31:6)

"Be strong and courageous. Do not be afraid or terrified because of them, for the Lord your God goes with you; he will never leave you nor forsake you."

Today, I was reminded of my past vision. I was in an elevator with a crowd full of people from the second floor (wanting to get to the first). I usually take the stairs if there are a few floors to walk. We went up instead of down. God said "I have changed your directions to trick the enemy". We got to the third floor, jerking hard, went down to the second floor even harder as we hit the first floor. Suddenly, I was in a cargo train with the same people from the elevator. I thought, I am trapped with the wrong people and confined to one space. But GOD said "you will never be trapped or confined because I am who I am....I am everywhere".

People were yelling and trying to get the train to stop. Part of the cargo door was closing in on us. People were trying to hold the door back or trying to level the cargo so it would stop moving. God said, "There will be people in your life trying to hold you back. Do not fear, for I will move people out of your life that will hinder my purpose for you. I pushed a man's back in front of me (out of fear) then he turned around and gave this look as to stop pushing him. GOD said there is a man in your way and you know who he is."

I stopped then another train appeared then I started praying that the cargo should stop and it did. GOD said prayer prevents things immediately in the supernatural realm. It might take time to reach you on earth but I am always working." I remember screaming "I'm getting out of here"! God said "I will always give you an escape." But when you are tempted, he will also provide a way out so that you can endure it (1 Corinthians 10:13). A window appeared to the left and I pulled it opened and jumped out.

I started walking quickly along the train tracks and saw a woman with a disappointed look on her face (she was sad because she missed the elevator or train). I thought to myself. I have to get off these tracks and she doesn't know how lucky she was. God said "when I see you taking the wrong path I will guide you back. We all, like sheep, have gone astray, each of us has turned to our own way; and the Lord has laid on him the iniquity of us all (Isaiah 53:6). There are some people I will send in your direction that you must guide as well."

I drank 13 cups of water and 3 cups of smoothie. I rehearsed five of my choreographed dance pieces for 2 hours.

YOUR EXPERIENCE

DAY 23

(Ecclesiastes 11:5)

"As you do not know the path of the wind, or how the body is formed[a] in a mother's womb, so you cannot understand the work of God, the Maker of all things."

Today I was reminded of a name..." Christiana Swanson". Her name came to me a few months ago. I didn't think I would meet her, but little did I know God has a plan. I was curious so I looked on the internet to see if I could find her. I found many of course, but felt like none of them were the right Christian Swanson.

There are mysterious ways in which God works, most of the visions you receive today may be useful in the future, but one thing is certain, whatever God says, it must surely come to pass. But I the Lord will speak what I will, and it shall be fulfilled without delay. For in your days, you rebellious people, I will fulfill whatever I say, declares the Sovereign Lord (Ezekiel 12:25).

 A month later I met a Christiana. Her last name was not Swanson but she was praying to be married soon. I rejoiced with her when I told her that GOD revealed her to me and believed soon she will meet her husband. Will his last name be Swanson? For I am going to do something in your days that you would not believe, even if you were told (Habakkuk 1:5)

I drank 18 cups of water, 2 cups of green tea. I did 50 sit ups, 20 jumping jacks and walked for one hour.

YOUR EXPERIENCE

DAY 24

"And God has placed in the church first of all apostles, second prophets, third teachers, then miracles, then gifts of healing, of helping, of guidance, and of different kinds of tongues. Are all apostles? Are all prophets? Are all teachers? Do all work miracles? Do all have gifts of healing? Do all speak in tongues? Do all interpret? Now eagerly desire the greater gifts."

Today, I was reminded again of my gift of sight. Before I left the ministry, I saw a baby spirit on one of my friends while dancing in church. After rehearsal, I told her what I saw and she rebuked me because she did not want any more children. This would have been baby number five for them. I thought to myself, I thought children were blessings so isn't it wonderful if you have many? I couldn't relate because I did not have any yet. Children are a heritage from the Lord, offspring a reward from him (Psalms 127:3). I smiled at her and said well I can only tell you what I saw.

I was away for almost a year and when I returned, she quickly walked over to me and joyfully said I have been waiting for so many months to get you. I looked at her belly and she was almost 9 months far along. She would have her baby the following week. Now to him who is able to do immeasurably more than all we ask or imagine, according to his power that is at work within us (Ephesians 3:20). I laughed joyously with her and was so excited for her. The way God works are beyond human expectation.

I drank 18 cups of water, 2 cups of green tea. I did 50 sit ups, 20 jumping jacks and walked for one hour.

YOUR EXPERIENCE

DAY 25

Isaiah 61:3

To console those who mourn in Zion, to give them beauty for ashes, the oil of joy for mourning, the garment of praise for the spirit of heaviness; that they may be called trees of righteousness, the planting of the LORD, that He may be glorified." –

Today, being the 25th day of my fast, I was exhausted. I did not work out or anything because I was really weak. I found myself falling asleep off and on through out the day. The last nap I took, I woke to a demon watching me. Before I opened my mouth, the demon left my house. It was afraid and that's what I want them all to be. But I am not sure if it was afraid of Jesus Christ in me and perhaps it was afraid of what I was about to say. Demons know we have authority over them, but they want you to think we do not.

I immediately prayed that it does not return with the authority of Jesus Christ. GOD told me people and entities are always watching you but now you are aware. Always be on guard and wear the full armor of praise.

"Finally, be strong in the Lord and in his mighty power. Put on the full armor of God, so that you can take your stand against the devil's schemes. For our struggle is not against flesh and blood, but against the rulers, against the authorities, against the powers of this dark world and against the spiritual forces of evil in the heavenly realms" (Ephesians 6:10-12).

I drank 16 cups of water, 2 cups of green tea and 2 cups of smoothie. I did 50 sit ups, 20 jumping jacks and walked for one hour.

YOUR EXPERIENCE

DAY 26

(1 Timothy 6:17-19)

"Command those who are rich in this present world not to be arrogant nor to put their hope in wealth, which is so uncertain, but to put their hope in God, who richly provides us with everything for our enjoyment. Command them to do good, to be rich in good deeds, and to be generous and willing to share. In this way they will lay up treasure for themselves as a firm foundation for the coming age, so that they may take hold of the life that is truly life."

Today, I was reminded of another vision. My husband and I were walking into a hugh car lot with thousands of cars. What actually amazed me was that, we were giving away brand new cars to many people. There are thousands of people outside who were waiting on us to open the doors. We arrive an hour before the event at the side door.

In the vision, I noticed that I was seven months pregnant, holding our little girl by my side hip, and I held my son's hand firmly in my left hand. My husband was carrying our new baby girl who was almost able to walk but not yet. He took our other little girl by my right hip as I said she is getting too heavy. My husband said, "I told you to put her down or give her to me". I was so excited about the event and couldn't wait to start helping so many people get cars for free. "Give to him who ask thee and from him who borrowed from thee not turn away" (Matthew 5:42).

I drank 17 cups of water, 2 cups of green tea, 4 cups of smoothie. I danced to random songs for praise and worship for 3 hours.

YOUR EXPERIENCE

DAY 27

(Luke 15:7)

"I tell you that in the same way there will be more rejoicing in heaven over one sinner who repents than over ninety-nine righteous persons who do not need to repent."

I usually go through my list of people I pray for: my husband, family, and friends...sometimes myself, and whoever drops in my spirit. But this time around, the last person who dropped in my spirit was a celebrity. As I prayed for his salvation and being freed from cults, I saw myself traveling through a demonic dimension. As I was going through, demons were trying to snatch me and kill me but as always I have the holy spirit and angels traveling with me. The angel of the Lord encamps around those who fear him, and he delivers them (Psalm 34:7).

I was in a room that was dark and demons were surrounding him as he was in the center of the circle. Outside of the circle stood for angels of the Lord. He stood trapped in a box were his feet were bond. There was sacrificed blood all around the circle to hold him captive. There were contracts under his feet in the box. He was like a statue, dead, but he was aware of the surroundings.

As I returned, I cried out to the Lord, "Why are your angels just standing there?" GOD said, "They are waiting on my word. I cannot move unless I hear my word. My word is alive and will work on my command." The Spirit gives life; the flesh counts for nothing. The words I have spoken to you, they are full of the Spirit and life. (John 6:63).

Then GOD showed me the celebrity's heart with a mustard seed inside it. So there is hope and so I prayed that the mustard seed of faith is not plucked out but continues to grow as I pray in the gap for him.

I had 12 cups of water, 2 cups of coco, 2 cups of green tea. I did my warm, cardio, and cool down routine when I made up while teaching a dance class earlier this year. It is usually one hour.

YOUR EXPERIENCE

DAY 28

(Mark 11:22-24)

"And Jesus answered them, "Have faith in God. Truly, I say to you, whoever says to this mountain, 'Be taken up and thrown into the sea,' and does not doubt in his heart, but believes that what he says will come to pass, it will be done for him. Therefore, I tell you, whatever you ask in prayer, believe that you have received it, and it will be yours."

As I was praying, I was thinking about all the desires of my heart and how they have not come to past. GOD said "It grieves me when you don't believe." I was struck with repentance and cried out for more faith. I was filled with an unshakable faith. Trust in the Lord with all your heart, and do not lean on your own understanding. In all your ways acknowledge him, and he will make straight your paths (Proverbs 3:5-6). No matter what I see, GOD will do it. "Be still, and know that I am God. I will be exalted among the nations; I will be exalted in the earth!"(Psalm 46:10).

I had 12 cups of water, 2 cups of coco, 2 cups of green tea. I danced before the Lord with my favorite song list for an hour.

YOUR EXPERIENCE

DAY 29

(Matthew 17:20)

"He replied, "Because you have so little faith. Truly I tell you, if you have faith as small as a mustard seed, you can say to this mountain, 'Move from here to there,' and it will move. Nothing will be impossible for you".

On the 29th day, God did an amazing change in my spiritual life. As I was praying, God said "your faith will be uncontainable." He showed me a broken pink big bowl and inside was faith. It continued to grow to an extent that the bowl broke open. For no matter how many promises God has made, they are "Yes" in Christ. And so through him the "Amen" is spoken by us to the glory of God (2 Corinthians 1:20)

My faith grew so much that it reached the atmosphere and therefore had broken all limits and boundaries.

I had 12 cups of water, 2 cups of coco, 2 cups of green tea. I dance before the Lord with my favorite song list for an hour.

YOUR EXPERIENCE

DAY 30

(Ephesians 2:10)

"We are God's workmanship, created in Christ Jesus for good works, which God prepared beforehand that we should walk in them."

Today in prayer, I saw a long dark road with demons along the side but were stopped by angels to move. GOD spoke and said, "There are no more delays."

I'll be 45 years old next year, and it's amazing to me how years feel like days. I ponder how all of these years went by so quickly. It's hard while the Lord makes you wait. You would think Paul should have struggled as he remained in custody in Caesarea. The attention we get seems almost like an insignificant passing comment: "But after two years had exceeded, Felix became succeeded via Porcius Festus; and wishing to do the Jews a desire, Felix left Paul imprisoned." (Acts 24).

As Paul waited and prayed and prayed and waited, he must have questioned, "Why didn't God get me out of here right away?" God said, "Walk in the path I have set before you and you will reap all your rewards that I want to give you. "Thus says the LORD, "Stand by the ways and see and ask for the ancient paths, Where the good way is, and walk in it; And you will find rest for your souls" (Jeremiah 6:16).

Something broke off me because I felt freer than ever. I had 14 cups of water and 1 cup of green tea.

YOUR EXPERIENCE

DAY 31

(Isaiah 41:10)

"So do not fear, for I am with you; do not be dismayed, for I am your God. I will strengthen you and help you; I will uphold you with my righteous right hand".

Today preparing to dance, GOD told me "It is your dance before me that gives you strength as well." Are you the using your own strength? Use your trial and your struggles to rely greatly upon the of God.

God provides his children with physical and spiritual strength in the time of need. God has given us endurance to stay in captivity for years. We might not know the reason, but I trust him to always bring me out.

I heard about a woman who was kidnapped and was bond by chains. During that time God was preserving her so she could escape. He gave her strategies to survive and a plan of escape. She was able to get the chains off and escape. God can destroy bodily chains, so surely he can destroy spiritual chains. Do not under estimate the power of God because he can help you in any situation just like he as always helped me. I will therefore that men pray everywhere, lifting up holy hands, without wrath and doubting (1 Timothy 2:8).

Our loving Father desires us to completely depend upon Him and not ourselves. God said, "Haven't you noticed when you are weak, I am strong. When you have no strength to pray or dance, I give it to you". The Lord is my strength and my song; he has given me victory (Exodus 15:2).

I drank 28 cups of water and 5 cups of smoothie. I danced four hours today with random songs.

YOUR EXPERIENCE

DAY 32

(2 Corinthians 12:9-10)

"But he said to me, "My grace is sufficient for you, for my power is made perfect in weakness." Therefore I will boast all the more gladly about my weaknesses, so that Christ's power may rest on me. 10 That is why, for Christ's sake, I delight in weaknesses, in insults, in hardships, in persecutions, in difficulties. For when I am weak, then I am strong."

God reminded me that it is all about preparation. The concordances imply that the word "preparation" happens only two times within the vintage testimony, once in (1Chronicles 22:5), where it was used within the ordinary sense "to make coaching," and as soon as in (Nahum 2:3), "within the day of his practice," each of them translating the equal Hebrew root and requiring no unique clarification.

In (Ephesians 6:15), the apostle speaks of the gadget of the Christian as inclusive of the "toes shod with the practice of the gospel of peace," which means that, according to Thayer, "with the promptitude and alacrity which the gospel produces."

The word occurs with technical significance ("the preparation") in the gospel narratives of the crucifixion, translating the Greek paraskeue (Matthew 27:62; Mark 15:42; Luke 23:54; John 19:14,31,42). It is used as a technical time period indicating the day of the guidance for the Sabbath, this is, the evening of Friday. This is its use in Josephus, Ant, XVI, vi, 2, and possibly inside the Synoptics. Later its use appears to have been extended to indicate regularly the sixth day (Friday) of each week. So inside the Didache, viii and the Martyrdom of Polycarp, vii.

I drank 10 cups of water, 2 cups of green tea, and 1 cup of smoothie. I walked two miles today.

YOUR EXPERIENCE

DAY 33

(John 8:36)

"So if the Son sets you free, you will be free indeed."

In prayer today, I saw myself wrapped with chains. GOD took them off and then I tried to put them back on. The Lord said,"I set you free but you are trying to go back to slavery. I have set the captive free so walk in your freedom and do not be bond again. I was free from my addictions. But now that you have been set free from sin and become slaves to God, the benefit you reap leads to holiness, and the result is eternal life (Romans 6:22).

I was reminded that some demons leave after prayer and some leave after prayer and fasting. It depends on which kind of demon you are dealing with (what kind of power). But the power that the enemy and demons have is no match to Jesus. Jesus have given his believers authority over all the enemy and cohorts. Then Jesus came to them and said, "All authority in heaven and on earth has been given to me (Matthew 28:18). What I had been feeling was confirmation, the Lord had delivered me from ungodly habits. I was no longer addicted to sugar. I no longer had OCD of germs.

I had 14 cups of water. I rehearsed 5 songs that choreographed for two hours for my fitness.

YOUR EXPERIENCE

DAY 34

(Matthew 19:6)

"So they are no longer two, but one flesh. Therefore, what God has joined together, let no one separate."

God told me that he loves when I pray to him for help because that is what he does best. If there is a miracle I need, he will do it because he will get the glory (1 Peter 5:12).

While I was mopping the middle hallway, I saw a chicken feet on my husband's door. I was told that Satan is trying to get a foot in our marriage and I need to cut it off. I immediately started to pray and go in spiritual warfare for my husband and our marriage.

The enemies are against marriages because it is ordained by GOD. So if there is a battle that must take place to fight for our marriage then there will be a fight! I am a warrior physically and spiritually. I will not accept defeat. My husband and I must continue to pray through challenges and difficulties to see God's glory and what he wants to reveal in us. I thank God for my spouse daily and I know our marriage is not based on a worldly vision but on the word vision. "Therefore, a man shall leave his father and his mother and hold fast to his wife, and they shall become one flesh. (Genesis 2:24).

Hours later, the chicken foot was no longer on the door and it has not returned.

I had 12 cups of water and 3 cups of coco.

YOUR EXPERIENCE

DAY 35

(Hebrews 12:2)

"fixing our eyes on Jesus, the pioneer and perfecter of faith. For the joy set before him he endured the cross, scorning its shame, and sat down at the right hand of the throne of God."

God reminded me of my lost earring. I woke up and went to the sink to wash my face, then I saw my lost heart golden earring I had lost a week ago. I was saddened that I lost it and remember praying to Lord about it, and he assured me that he would return it to me.

These were my favorite earrings because they were real gold and my mother bought them for me. I had bothered my mother for a year to buy those earrings. I thought I lost it in my bedroom where all my other jewelries were boxed. I made a mess of my bedroom looking for my heart gold earring.

God said, " I am restoring what you thought was lost. You were looking in the wrong place to find things, always look to me. They looked to Him and were radiant, And their faces will never be ashamed (Psalm 34:5). God is so merciful and wonderful, even when you don't trust him fully, He restores anyway.

I had 10 cups of water and 1 smoothie. I rehearsed 5 songs that choreographed for two hours for my fitness.

YOUR EXPERIENCE

DAY 36

(Exodus 9:16)

"But I have raised you up for this very purpose, that I might show you my power and that my name might be proclaimed in all the earth".

This is the home stretch...I am feeling pretty good and I realized I was filled with more energy than ever. I am curious about what kinds of foods I will no longer like. "Many are the plans in a person's heart, but it is the Lord's purpose that prevails" (Proverbs 19:21).

In prayer, I became pregnant with purpose. I am always carrying a baby (purpose) for someone. I released two but I am carrying nine purposes in total. "Therefore, my dear friends, as you have always obeyed—not only in my presence, but now much more in my absence—continue to work out your salvation with fear and trembling, for it is God who works in you to will and to act in order to fulfill his good purpose" (Philippians 2:12-13).

I drank 18 cups of water and 3 cups of smoothie. I danced before the lord for two hours today

YOUR EXPERIENCE

DAY 37

(Psalm 139:1-6)

"Lord, you have examined me and know all about me. You know when I sit down and when I get up. You know my thoughts before I think them. You know where I go and where I lie down. You know everything I do. Lord, even before I say a word, you already know it. You are all around me—in front and in back— and have put your hand on me. Your knowledge is amazing to me; it is more than I can understand."

In prayer, GOD said "ask me anything and I will answer". I got nervous because there were many questions that I wanted to ask and I am not even sure of the one to ask first.

When I thought of the question within me, GOD began to answer me but then I interrupted him and said never mind Lord. My human brain cannot accept the answer, maybe later on, I will be ready to hear the answers. GOD laughed and said ok. Oh, the depth of the riches of the wisdom and knowledge of God!. How unsearchable his judgments, and his paths beyond tracing out! "Who has known the mind of the Lord? Or who has been his counselor?" (Romans 11:33-34).

I asked a simple question and he answered me before I could finish my thought. I love it when he does that!

I had 18 cups of water and 2 cups of green tea.

YOUR EXPERIENCE

DAY 38

(2 Corinthians 10:3-5)

"For though we live in the world, we do not wage war as the world does. The weapons we fight with are not the weapons of the world. On the contrary, they have divine power to demolish strongholds. We demolish arguments and every pretension that sets itself up against the knowledge of God, and we take captive every thought to make it obedient to Christ."

Today, I began thanking the Lord for everything. I began praying in tongues and I felt strongholds breaking off from my past relationships. I still had baggage because I was hurt in two serious relationships and was still holding on to that hurt. I no longer wanted anything to interfere in my marriage. I went in spiritual warfare and I felt the contracts get destroyed.

As soon as I said Amen. I heard and saw demons plotting to have me sign more contracts. I quickly rebuked them and the leader of the group said, "I see you." I replied, "So and I see you. What did I tell your friends before, do not talk to me!" I started speaking in tongues and heard my voice change. I saw the demons fall to hell.

I drank 17 cups of water and 2 cups of green tea. I did a fitness routine I learned earlier that year for a about an hour.

YOUR EXPERIENCE

DAY 39

(Romans 5:2-4)

"Through whom we have gained access by faith into this grace in which we now stand. And we boast in the hope of the glory of God. Not only so, but we also glory in our sufferings, because we know that suffering produces perseverance; perseverance, character; and character, hope."

God said "You have been truly patient and I am proud of you. You have shown me you truly want my best for you. I want to give you which you may not get in your Christian walk of faith without persistence".

God gave me something and I am not sure what it is because he has not revealed it to me. However, I do know it's a treasure from Heaven.

Many human beings in scripture made bad alternatives due to their lack of staying patient. Acquainted names are Saul, Moses, and Samson. In case you are not persistence, you're going to make unwise decisions.

Many believers are dealing with the consequences of unwise decisions. God does intervenes in situations; however, we should not fight with God to do our own will. He is attempting to protect us from things we can not see or are unaware of. The Lord is perfect and we must wait for his perfect timing. His timing can seem long and other times it will feel quick.

Instead he is patient with you, not wanting anyone to perish, but everyone to come to repentance (2 Peter 3:9).

Impatience draws us far from God. Staying patient attracts us in the direction of God revealing a heart that trusts and is confident in the Lord.

God remembers what he has promised us and I believe it will not be anything temporary, false, or anything that is connected to trouble. The godly are rescued from trouble, and it falls on the wicked instead (Proverbs 11:8).

I drank 15 cups of water and 4 cups of green tea. I started a new dance and choreographed the first 5 minutes of it for 2 hours.

YOUR EXPERIENCE

DAY 40

(2 Timothy 4:7-8)

"I have fought the good fight, I have finished the race, I have kept the faith. Now there is in store for me the crown of righteousness, which the Lord, the righteous Judge, will award to me on that day—and not only to me, but also to all who have longed for his appearing."

In prayer, I thanked GOD for letting me get through the 40 days and 40 nights of fasting and for changing my life. I am free from addictions, wrong patterns of thinking, and soul ties. Specifically, I was delivered from the following demons: spirit of self-worthlessness, spirit of guilt, spirit of perfectionism, spirit of doubt, spirit of hopelessness, spirit of perversion, spirit of depression, and spirit of control. I decided to incorporate fasting every week. I would fast for a few days every week for now on and being guided by Jesus' instructions on what to fast.

I promised never to allow the enemy to trick me again. In order that satan might not outwit us. For we are not unaware of his schemes (2 Corinthians 2:11).

The only meat I eat officially is fish. My love for fruit and vegetables have grown. I cannot eat a lot of cheese, salt, sweets because it makes me sick now. I don't have one blemish on my face and I lost 17 pounds. I now have a closer relationship with Jesus. My gifts have grown and Jesus revealed new ones. I am excited about my future and the lives that I can help with my experience.

YOUR EXPERIENCE

SMOOTHIES

Pear Spinach Smoothie

2 medium Bartlett pears

½ lime

1 medium banana

2 C. red grapes

1 C. water

½ bunch spinach

Blend all ingredients together except spinach until smooth. Add spinach and blend.

Grape Kiwi Smoothie

2 C. red grapes

4 medium kiwis

2 medium bananas

1 C. water

Small handful of arugula

8 leaves kale

Blend all ingredients together except arugula and kale until smooth. Add arugula and kale and blend.

Pear Raspberry Smoothie

2 medium Bartlett pears

1 C. raspberries

3 oz spinach

Water if needed or desired

Blend all ingredients together
except spinach until smooth. Add spinach and blend.

Green Pineapple Smoothie

1 medium banana

1 C. red grapes

10 oz pineapple

5 oz spinach

2 large ribs of celery

Water if needed or desired

Blend all ingredients together except spinach until smooth.
Add spinach and blend.

Pineapple Raspberry Smoothie

1 medium banana

10 oz pineapple

6 oz raspberries

Blend all ingredients together adding water as needed.

Pear Orange Banana Smoothie

1 medium banana

3 Bartlett pears

1 medium orange

1 C. water

Blend all ingredients together.

Add 3 oz. spinach, romaine or other greens for a green smoothie.

Red Raspberry Smoothie

1 medium banana

3 Bartlett pears

6 oz raspberries

Blend all ingredients together

Purple Pear Smoothie

1 medium banana

3 Bartlett pears

6 oz blackberries

Blend all ingredients together

Strawberry Smoothie

2 medium bananas

1 C. red grapes

1 lb. strawberries

2 oranges

5 oz spinach

Blend all ingredients together except spinach

Until smooth. Add spinach and blend

Peachy Keen Smoothie

2 peaches

2 oranges

1 C, red grapes

Blend all together.

Blackberry Grape Smoothie

1 medium banana

1½ C. red grapes

6 0z. blackberries

2 oranges'

Blend all ingredients together

Orange Mango Smoothie

2 mangos

2 oranges

1 banana

Blend all ingredients together. This is

Thick smoothie, omit banana for thinner consistency

YOUR FAST GOALS

TESTIMONIES

I wanted to try the 40 days and 40 nights fast to try to experience what Jesus went through. I followed Jesus' steps and went through hell, I was under attack. The worst possible things happened to me...but my final step led me back to Jesus. I was dealing with a little of doubt about who Jesus really was, but after the fast, Jesus showed me himself. I experienced Jesus like never before and he took away all doubt. I recommitted my life back to Christ after my fast and I am looking forward getting closer to him. I choose to only drink water during my fast. I occasionally, ate snack food like granola bar and smoothie once a day for work purposes. I lost 15 pounds and trying to keep the weight off. I drink more water daily and love it.

-Theresa B.

I was delivered from the spirit of gluttony and spirit of masturbation. During the fast, Jesus told me that I was punishing myself for things I wanted to happen in my life but did not. I was disappointed in several events in my life including messing up on my fast. I choose to eat one meal a day, but ended up eating two meals during my second week. I quickly asked for repentance and ended the fast strong while staying on track. God was showing me how I overate and masturbated to try to feel a void. All I really felt afterwards, was more loneliness and disappointment.

That's because only Jesus can feel the voids in your life. He taught me how to rely on him and no one else. He showed me how he died just for me and you. I was given an overwhelming love and identity in him. I know I will never be the same.

-Sarah M.

I choose to give up all pastries. I am a baker at a few restaurants, and I knew giving up pastries would be a definite sacrifice. It was a challenge and at times I felt like I was dying. But it was just the sugar withdrawal. I had to call off work for a few days because the temptation was strong.

I was always an insecure child growing up. My mother was verbal abusive, and I never knew how much I was valued until I found Jesus. I was saved at a young age, but was curious about things of the world. I ended up with the wrong crowd of people who encouraged me to try drugs. I became addicted to a few types of drugs. I have been doing drugs for about ten years. I thought it was ok because they were prescription drugs. But I now know how the devil tricked me into believing that lie. After my fast, I can honestly say, I am free from all drug addictions. Sometimes, I still go through withdraws, but its' been another 40 days since I used drugs. I lost 30 pounds and no longer eat pastries everyday because I now work at healthier restaurants. Additionally, I am a gluten free eater. God delivered me from the spirit of addiction, the spirit of jealousy, spirit of depression, and spirit of unforgiveness. I was able to forgive my mom and we are working on mending our relationship.

-Darnell S.

I choose to eat no food for my fast, but liquids only. I was married at a young age and my husband and I were virgins. We really did not know a lot about sex and thought it would be ok to watch pornography together. Well, my husband stopped watching it, but I continued and became addicted to it. I would try to copy what some of the women did, but my husband wasn't pleased because he felt that I was out of character. He would question me about my actions and I would just lie. During my fast, God delivered me from pornography. I repented to Jesus and my husband and there was no condemnation. I knew Jesus would forgive me, but I was not sure about my husband. I was so happy when he did and today we have the best sex life because we allowed only GOD in our marriage bed.

-Tamika H.

YOUR TESTIMONIES

Printed in Great Britain
by Amazon

43233225R00071